Brews and Bray

A Guide to Starting a Brewery with a Donkey

By
Cory Mellor & Bryan Mellor

Chapter 1: Brewing Basics
- Understanding the brewing process: Ingredients, equipment, and techniques.
- Types of beer: Ales, lagers, stouts, and more.
- Recipe development: Creating unique and appealing flavors.

Chapter 2: The Donkey's Role
- Introducing your donkey: Choosing the right breed and temperament.
- Utilizing donkey power: Transporting ingredients, milling grains, and more.
- Donkey care and training: Health, grooming, and handling.

Chapter 3: Setting Up Your Brewery
- Location and space considerations: Finding the perfect spot for your brewery.

- Designing the brewery layout: Incorporating space for the donkey's activities.
- Equipment selection: Brewhouse, fermentation vessels, and packaging machinery.

Chapter 4: Donkey-Driven Brewing
- Grain milling with a donkey-powered mill.
- Mixing and mashing: Harnessing donkey energy for the process.
- Brewing efficiency and sustainability: The environmental benefits of donkey power.

Chapter 5: Donkey Branding and Marketing
- Incorporating the donkey into your brewery's branding and story.
- Crafting a unique identity: Labels, logos, and merchandise.
- Donkey-themed events: Engaging customers and building community.

Chapter 6: Donkey Welfare and Regulations
- Ensuring the well-being of your donkey: Proper diet, shelter, and exercise.
- Legal and ethical considerations: Animal welfare regulations and permits.
- Building positive relationships: Involving local animal advocacy groups.

Chapter 7: Navigating Challenges
- Handling unexpected situations: Health issues, weather, and more.
- Balancing workloads: Donkey capabilities and avoiding overexertion.
- Evolving your brewery: Scaling up and adapting your processes.

Chapter 8: Success Stories
- Profiles of successful breweries with animal involvement.
- Lessons learned and insights from experienced brewmasters.
- Donkey-powered innovations: Pioneering new techniques in brewing.

Chapter 1: Brewing Basics

Brewing beer is an art that spans centuries, evolving from ancient traditions to modern techniques. This chapter will introduce you to the fundamental aspects of brewing beer and provide an understanding of the brewing process. As you embark on your journey to start a brewery with a donkey, mastering these basics will be essential.

Section 1: Understanding the Brewing Process

Brewing beer involves transforming a handful of simple ingredients into a flavorful and satisfying beverage. These ingredients include water, malted grains, hops, and yeast. Here's a brief overview of the brewing process:

1. Malting: Malted grains (usually barley) are soaked, germinated, and dried to develop enzymes that convert starches into fermentable sugars.

2. Mashing: The malted grains are mixed with hot water in a process called mashing. This allows enzymes to break down the starches into sugars, creating a sweet liquid known as wort.

3. Boiling: The wort is brought to a boil and hops are added. Hops contribute bitterness, flavor, and aroma to the beer. The boiling process also sterilizes the wort.

4. Cooling and Fermentation: After boiling, the wort is rapidly cooled and transferred to a fermentation vessel. Yeast is added, and fermentation begins. Yeast consumes the sugars in the wort, producing alcohol and carbon dioxide.

5. Conditioning: Once fermentation is complete, the beer is allowed to mature. This helps develop its flavor profile and allows any undesirable compounds to settle out.

6. Packaging: The beer is filtered, carbonated, and packaged in bottles, cans, or kegs for distribution and consumption.

Section 2: Types of Beer

There's a wide variety of beer styles, each with its own unique characteristics and flavor profiles. Some popular styles include ales, lagers, stouts, porters, and IPAs (India Pale Ales). Understanding the nuances of these styles will help you create a diverse and appealing beer menu for your donkey-assisted brewery.

Section 3: Recipe Development

Crafting your own beer recipes is where creativity truly shines. A successful brewery offers a range of flavors to cater to different preferences. Here's a simplified process for recipe development:

1. Select Your Style: Choose the style of beer you want to brew, considering factors like color, flavor, and aroma.

2. Malt Selection: Different malts contribute different flavors and colors. Experiment with various malt combinations.

3. Hop Selection: Hops impact bitterness and aroma. Choose hops that complement your chosen style.

4. Yeast Choice: Yeast strains have a significant influence on the beer's flavor and aroma. Different strains ferment at different temperatures and produce varying levels of esters and phenols.

5. Balance and Complexity: Strive for a balanced flavor profile. Consider the interplay between malt sweetness, hop bitterness, and yeast characteristics.

6. Experimentation: Don't be afraid to experiment with unconventional ingredients or techniques to create unique brews that set your brewery apart.

As you begin your journey into the world of brewing, remember that practice makes perfect. Take the time to refine your techniques and recipes, and always be open to learning from both successes and setbacks. With a solid understanding of the brewing process, you're ready to delve into the next chapters that explore how to incorporate a donkey into your brewery operations.

Chapter 2: The Donkey's Role

Introducing a donkey into your brewery operations is a unique and innovative approach that adds both charm and practicality. In this chapter, we'll delve into the considerations for choosing the right donkey, utilizing its power, and ensuring its well-being.

Section 1: Choosing the Right Donkey

Selecting the appropriate donkey for your brewery requires careful consideration. Different donkey breeds and temperaments can affect how well the animal adapts to brewery activities. Here are some factors to keep in mind:

1. Breed: Some donkey breeds are more suited for heavy work, while others are better companions. Research breeds that have a history of being used in agricultural and labor-intensive tasks.

2. Temperament: A donkey's personality plays a crucial role. Look for a donkey that is calm, cooperative, and social. Avoid overly aggressive or skittish individuals.

3. Size: Consider the size of your brewery space and the tasks the donkey will perform. A donkey that is too large or small might not be as effective in carrying out its duties.

4. Health: Ensure that the donkey is in good health. A veterinary examination can help identify any pre-existing conditions that might affect its ability to work.

Section 2: Utilizing Donkey Power

Donkeys have historically been used as reliable and strong work animals. Incorporating a donkey into your brewery operations can have numerous benefits:

1. Transporting Ingredients: Donkeys can help transport bags of malted grains, hops, and other brewing ingredients around the brewery, reducing the need for manual labor or machinery.

2. Grain Milling: Donkeys can be trained to power grain mills. Their circular motion can turn the millstones, grinding the grains for brewing.

3. Mashing Assistance: Donkeys can be harnessed to assist with stirring and mashing the grain during the brewing process, saving energy and time.

4. Promotional Activities: A friendly and well-trained donkey can attract customers and enhance the brewery's ambiance. Donkey-themed events can create memorable experiences.

Section 3: Donkey Care and Training

Ensuring the well-being of your donkey is paramount. A happy and healthy donkey will be more cooperative and effective in brewery tasks. Here are some tips for caring and training:

1. Shelter: Provide adequate shelter to protect the donkey from extreme weather conditions.

2. Diet: Consult with a veterinarian to develop a balanced diet that meets the donkey's nutritional needs.

3. Exercise: Regular exercise is essential for the donkey's physical and mental well-being. Incorporate regular walks and activities into its routine.

4. Training: Training should be positive, reward-based, and consistent. Teach the donkey basic commands and acclimate it to the brewery environment.

Remember that donkeys are social animals, and building a bond of trust with your donkey is crucial. Spend time interacting with the animal and providing it with positive experiences. A well-cared-for and content donkey will contribute not only to the brewery's operations but also to its overall atmosphere.

As you move forward in your journey of starting a brewery with a donkey, the next chapter will focus on practical considerations for setting up your brewery space to accommodate your new four-legged team member.

Chapter 3: Setting Up Your Brewery

Creating a functional and welcoming space for both your brewing operations and your donkey is key to the success of your brewery. In this chapter, we'll explore the considerations for selecting the right location, designing the brewery layout, and choosing the necessary equipment to harmoniously incorporate your donkey into the operation.

Section 1: Choosing the Right Location

Selecting an appropriate location for your donkey-assisted brewery requires careful thought. Consider the following factors:

1. Space: Ensure you have enough space to accommodate both the brewing equipment and the donkey's activities. A larger space might be necessary to prevent overcrowding.

2. Accessibility: Choose a location that's easily accessible for both customers and suppliers. Adequate parking and transportation options are essential.

3. Zoning and Regulations: Research local zoning regulations and any permits required for running a brewery and keeping animals on the premises.

Section 2: Designing the Brewery Layout

Efficient utilization of space is essential for a functional brewery. Here's how you can design your layout to incorporate the donkey:

1. Donkey Area: Designate a comfortable and safe area for the donkey within the brewery. This area should include shelter, water, and a designated space for rest.

2. Brewing Space: Plan the layout of your brewing equipment, fermentation vessels, and packaging machinery to maximize workflow efficiency.

3. Donkey Pathways: Create clear pathways for the donkey to move around the brewery without causing obstructions. These pathways should be designed to ensure the donkey's safety.

Section 3: Equipment Selection

Choosing the right brewing equipment is crucial for producing high-quality beer efficiently. Additionally, you'll need to select equipment that can accommodate the donkey's contributions. Consider the following:

1. Donkey-Powered Mill: Look for a suitable grain mill that can be powered by the donkey's circular motion. This will help with grain grinding during the brewing process.

2. Harnessing Equipment: Invest in appropriate harnessing equipment that allows you to safely attach the donkey to tasks like milling or stirring.

3. Brewing Equipment: Choose brewing equipment that aligns with your recipes and production scale. This includes brewhouses, fermentation vessels, and packaging machinery.

4. Storage: Allocate space for storing brewing ingredients, finished products, and equipment to ensure a tidy and organized brewery.

By carefully planning and designing your brewery space, you'll be able to create a harmonious environment where brewing and donkey-assisted activities can coexist seamlessly. In the next chapter, we'll explore the practical aspects of incorporating the donkey into the brewing process, from grain milling to mashing.

Chapter 4: Donkey-Driven Brewing

Incorporating a donkey into the brewing process adds a unique and eco-friendly dimension to your operations. This chapter will delve into how you can harness the power of your donkey for various brewing tasks, making your brewery both efficient and charming.

Section 1: Grain Milling with a Donkey-Powered Mill

Donkeys have been used for centuries to power various types of mills, and your brewery can benefit from their strength for grain milling:

1. Setting Up the Mill: Invest in a donkey-powered grain mill that can efficiently grind malted grains. Set up the mill in an accessible area within the brewery.

2. Harnessing the Donkey: Train your donkey to become comfortable with the milling process. Attach the donkey to the mill using appropriate harnessing equipment.

3. Grain Grinding: As the donkey walks in circles, its circular motion will power the millstones, grinding the malted grains into the desired consistency.

4. Efficiency and Sustainability: Donkey-powered milling not only adds a unique element to your brewery but also contributes to your sustainability efforts by reducing reliance on electricity.

Section 2: Mixing and Mashing with Donkey Assistance

Donkeys can also play a role in the mashing process, where water and malted grains are mixed to create wort:

1. Donkey-Assisted Stirring: During the mashing process, the donkey can be harnessed to help stir the mash, ensuring even mixing of water and malt.

2. Balancing Workloads: Pay attention to the donkey's energy levels and the amount of effort required. Avoid overexerting the animal and provide breaks as needed.

3. Teamwork and Atmosphere: Incorporating the donkey in mashing adds an interactive and engaging element for visitors, enhancing their brewery experience.

Section 3: Brewing Efficiency and Sustainability

Donkey-powered activities contribute to a more sustainable and environmentally conscious brewery:

1. Reduced Energy Consumption: Donkey power reduces your reliance on electricity, lowering energy costs and minimizing your carbon footprint.

2. Educational Opportunities: Donkey-assisted brewing offers educational opportunities for visitors to learn about traditional methods and the benefits of sustainable practices.

3. Promotional Advantage: Highlight your brewery's commitment to sustainable practices and animal welfare as part of your marketing strategy.

As you introduce donkey-assisted tasks into your brewing process, always prioritize the well-being of the animal. Regular exercise, proper nutrition, and positive reinforcement training will ensure that your donkey remains happy and healthy while contributing to the brewery's success.

In the next chapter, we'll explore how to integrate your donkey into your brewery's branding and marketing strategies, creating a memorable and unique identity for your establishment.

Chapter 5: Donkey Branding and Marketing

Incorporating a donkey into your brewery offers a charming and distinctive element that can set your establishment apart from the rest. This chapter will guide you through the process of integrating your donkey into your brewery's branding and marketing efforts to create a memorable and engaging experience for your customers.

Section 1: Incorporating the Donkey into Your Brand

1. Tell Your Story: Craft a compelling narrative that explains how the donkey became a part of your brewery's identity. Share the reasons behind your choice and the positive impact it brings to your operations.

2. Logo and Imagery: Design a logo that features your donkey and reflects the essence of your brewery. Incorporate the donkey into promotional materials, signage, and merchandise.

3. Naming Opportunities : Consider giving your donkey a unique name that aligns with your brand's theme or the types of beer you produce. Playful and creative names can resonate with customers.

Section 2: Crafting a Unique Identity

1. Donkey-Themed Merchandise: Design and offer merchandise such as t-shirts, mugs, and keychains featuring your donkey and brewery logo. These items can serve as memorable souvenirs for your visitors.

2. Special Events: Organize donkey-themed events, such as "Donkey Days" or "Brews & Bray" gatherings. These events can include donkey-related activities, educational sessions, and brewery tours.

3. Social Media Engagement: Showcase your donkey's daily activities on social media platforms. Share behind-the-scenes glimpses of the donkey's contributions and interactions with visitors.

Section 3: Donkey-Themed Events and Engagement

1. Donkey Meet-and-Greets: Offer customers the opportunity to meet and interact with the donkey in a controlled and safe environment. This personal interaction can create lasting memories.

2. Donkey-Drawn Cart Rides: If feasible, consider offering short rides or tours around the brewery premises using a donkey-drawn cart. This can be a unique and family-friendly attraction.

3. Donkey-Powered Demonstrations: Hold demonstrations of the donkey's contributions to the brewing process. Explain the

historical significance of using animals in brewing while highlighting your innovative approach.

By incorporating the donkey into your branding and marketing efforts, you're not only creating a distinctive identity for your brewery but also fostering a sense of community and connection with your customers. The unique experiences you offer will become talking points and encourage repeat visits, ultimately contributing to the success of your donkey-assisted brewery.

In the next chapter, we'll discuss the importance of maintaining the welfare of your donkey and navigating any regulatory considerations to ensure a harmonious coexistence between the animal and your brewing operations.

Chapter 6: Donkey Welfare and Regulations

Ensuring the well-being of your donkey and complying with relevant regulations are essential aspects of running a successful donkey-assisted brewery. This chapter will guide you through the steps of caring for your donkey and navigating legal and ethical considerations.

Section 1: Ensuring Donkey Well-Being

1. Shelter and Comfort: Provide a sheltered area that protects the donkey from harsh weather conditions. Ensure that the shelter is well-ventilated and equipped with clean bedding.

2. Diet and Nutrition: Consult with a veterinarian to establish a balanced diet that meets the nutritional needs of your donkey. Provide fresh water at all times.

3. Exercise and Enrichment: Incorporate regular exercise and mental stimulation into the donkey's routine. Engage the donkey in activities that cater to its natural instincts, such as grazing and walking.

4. Healthcare: Schedule regular veterinary check-ups to monitor the donkey's health. Keep up with vaccinations, deworming, and hoof care.

Section 2: Legal and Ethical Considerations

1. Animal Welfare Regulations: Familiarize yourself with local and national regulations regarding animal welfare. Ensure that your donkey's living conditions and care meet or exceed the required standards.

2. Permits and Licensing: Depending on your location, you may need permits or licenses to keep animals on your brewery premises. Research and obtain the necessary documentation.

3. Animal Advocacy Groups: Establish positive relationships with local animal advocacy organizations. This can demonstrate your commitment to animal welfare and provide a resource for guidance.

Section 3: Building Positive Relationships

1. Community Engagement: Engage with your local community to educate them about your donkey-assisted brewery. Highlight the animal's role and contributions to brewing.

2. Educational Initiatives: Offer educational sessions or workshops about the historical significance of animals in brewing and the sustainable practices you've adopted.

3. Transparency: Be transparent with your customers about how you care for your donkey and ensure that it is treated with respect and kindness.

By prioritizing the welfare of your donkey and adhering to regulations, you create a positive environment that reflects your brewery's values and ethics. Customers who witness your commitment to animal welfare will likely appreciate your dedication and may become loyal patrons of your establishment.

In the final chapter, we'll discuss the challenges and rewards of running a donkey-assisted brewery, including tips for overcoming obstacles and evolving your brewery to meet changing demands.

Chapter 7: Navigating Challenges and Embracing Growth

Running a donkey-assisted brewery presents its own set of challenges and rewards. In this chapter, we'll explore how to navigate obstacles that may arise and capitalize on opportunities for growth and evolution.

Section 1: Handling Unexpected Situations

1. Health Concerns: Monitor your donkey's health closely. Address any health issues promptly and work with a veterinarian to ensure quick and effective treatment.

2. Weather Challenges: Extreme weather conditions can affect both your brewing operations and the well-being of your donkey. Have contingency plans in place for adverse weather.

3. Donkey Training: Continuously train your donkey to perform its tasks safely and effectively. Address any behavioral issues promptly to maintain a harmonious environment.

Section 2: Balancing Workloads and Well-Being

1. Workload Management: Pay attention to the donkey's energy levels and avoid overburdening it with tasks. Allow for breaks and rest periods.

2. Donkey-Driven Activities: Regularly assess which tasks are suitable for donkey involvement and adjust accordingly. Keep in mind that the donkey's well-being is paramount.

Section 3: Evolving Your Brewery

1. Scaling Up: As your brewery gains popularity, consider expanding your offerings and increasing production. Ensure that your donkey's contributions remain aligned with the increased demands.

2. Innovation: Continuously innovate and experiment with new brewing techniques and recipes. The donkey can become a symbol of your brewery's dedication to traditional methods while embracing innovation.

3. Community Engagement: Continue engaging with your community through events, workshops, and educational initiatives. Cultivate a loyal customer base by emphasizing the unique experiences your brewery offers.

4. Sustainability Initiatives: Explore additional ways to incorporate sustainable practices beyond donkey-assisted brewing. This could include sourcing local ingredients and minimizing waste.

Section 4: Celebrating Successes

1. Success Stories: Share success stories of how the donkey has contributed to your brewery's success. Highlight the positive impact on both your operations and the customer experience.

2. Customer Feedback: Listen to customer feedback and adapt based on their preferences. Encourage customers to share their experiences and memories related to the donkey.

3. Continuous Learning: Stay informed about industry trends and best practices. Attend workshops and conferences to learn from other brewers and animal-assisted businesses.

By embracing challenges as opportunities for growth and maintaining a commitment to the well-being of your donkey, you'll be well-positioned to succeed in the unique world of donkey-assisted brewing. Your brewery can become a symbol of innovation, sustainability, and community engagement while preserving traditional methods and forging a distinct identity.

In the final chapter, we'll reflect on the journey you've embarked upon and offer closing thoughts on the legacy of your donkey-assisted brewery.

Chapter 8: A Legacy of Tradition and Innovation

As you conclude this journey of running a donkey-assisted brewery, it's important to reflect on the path you've taken, the impact you've made, and the legacy you're leaving behind. This final chapter celebrates the culmination of your efforts and offers closing thoughts on the unique venture you've undertaken.

Section 1: Pioneering New Techniques

1. Brewing Traditions: Your brewery stands as a testament to the fusion of time-honored traditions and modern innovation. The donkey-assisted approach not only pays homage to historical practices but also pushes the boundaries of creativity.

2. Inspiration for Others: Your brewery's success can inspire others to explore unconventional methods in their brewing endeavors. By sharing your experiences, you contribute to the broader landscape of brewing innovation.

Section 2: A Symbol of Community and Connection

1. Creating Memories: Your donkey-assisted brewery has likely provided countless visitors with unique memories and experiences. The donkey's presence has enhanced customer engagement and community bonds.

2. Sustainable Values: Your commitment to sustainability and animal welfare serves as an example of responsible business practices. This legacy of ethical consideration can influence others to adopt similar approaches.

Section 3: Adapting and Evolving

1. Changing Demands: The brewing landscape is ever-evolving. Your ability to adapt your brewery to changing customer preferences and industry trends showcases your resilience and dedication.

2. Cultural Impact: By infusing the brewery experience with the charm of a donkey, you've added a distinctive cultural dimension to your community. Your brewery becomes not just a place to enjoy beer, but a part of local identity.

Section 4: Looking Forward

1. Continuing the Legacy: Even as you conclude this journey, your brewery's legacy lives on. It's up to you to ensure that the values, experiences, and relationships you've built endure beyond this moment.

2. Future Generations: Consider how your donkey-assisted brewery can serve as an educational platform for future generations. Your story can inspire aspiring brewers and animal enthusiasts alike.

As you close the chapter on your donkey-assisted brewery, remember that the impact you've made is significant. Your innovation, dedication, and willingness to embrace tradition have created a unique establishment that has touched the lives of many. Cheers to the journey you've undertaken, and may your legacy continue to thrive in the hearts and memories of those who have experienced the magic of your donkey-assisted brewery.

Thank You for Reading

As you close this book, we extend our heartfelt gratitude to you for taking the time to explore the concept of a donkey-assisted brewery. Your curiosity and interest in combining tradition, innovation, and a love for animals have led you through a remarkable journey. Whether you're considering starting your own brewery, seeking inspiration, or simply enjoying the imaginative exploration of this idea, we hope this book has provided valuable insights and sparked your imagination.

Remember that every endeavor begins with a spark of creativity, and your ability to transform ideas into reality is a testament to your ingenuity. Whether you're raising a glass to the future or contemplating the rich tapestry of the past, your journey is uniquely yours to embrace and shape.

Thank you for joining us on this imaginative journey. Cheers to your adventures, your dreams, and the joy of creating something truly extraordinary.

Warmest regards,

Cory and Bryan